African-American Heroes

Barack Obama

Stephen Feinstein

Enslow Elementary

an imprint of

E ‖‖ **Enslow Publishers, Inc.**

‖ USA

http://www.enslow.com

Words to Know

adventure—An exciting happening.

Hawaii (hu-WHY-ee)—A U.S. state made up of a group of islands in the Pacific Ocean.

Honolulu (ha-nuh-LOO-loo)—The capital city of Hawaii.

housing projects—Groups of apartment houses for poor people to live in.

Indonesia (in-doh-NEE-zha)—A country in Southeast Asia.

Jakarta (juh-CAR-tuh)—The capital city of Indonesia.

Kenya (KEN-yuh)—A country in East Africa bordering on the Indian Ocean.

Enslow Elementary, an imprint of Enslow Publishers, Inc.

Enslow Elementary® is a registered trademark of Enslow Publishers, Inc.

Library of Congress Cataloging-in-Publication Data
Feinstein, Stephen.
    Barack Obama / Stephen Feinstein.
        p. cm. — (African-American heroes)
    Summary: "An elementary biography of United States senator from Illinois Barack Obama; discusses his childhood, ethnic background, family, and career in politics"—Provided by publisher.
    Includes bibliographical references and index.
    ISBN-13: 978-0-7660-2893-7
    ISBN-10: 0-7660-2893-3
    1. Obama, Barack—Juvenile literature. 2. African American legislators—Biography—Juvenile literature. 3. Legislators—United States—Biography—Juvenile literature. 4. United States. Congress. Senate—Biography—Juvenile literature.
5. Presidential candidates—United States—Biography—Juvenile literature. 6. Racially mixed people—United States—Biography—Juvenile literature. I. Title.
    E901.1.O23F45 2008
    328.73092—dc22
    [B]   2007036363
Printed in the United States of America
10 9 8 7 6 5 4 3 2 1

Illustration Credits: AP/Wide World, pp. 1, 2, 3, 5, 10, 12, 13, 15, 16, 17, 18, 19, 20, 21, back cover; Enslow Publishers, Inc., pp. 4, 8, 11; Shutterstock, pp. 3, 6, 7, 9.

Cover Illustration: AP/Wide World.

 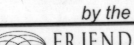

Contents

Chapter

1

Growing Up in Hawaii .... Page **4**

Chapter

2

Barry's Big Adventure .... Page **8**

Chapter

3

Barry Visits Africa .... Page **11**

Chapter

4

Barack Becomes a Senator .... Page **17**

Timeline | Learn More | Index
Page **22** | Page **23** | Page **24**

Chapter 1 Growing Up in Hawaii

Barack Obama was born on August 4, 1961, in **Honolulu**, **Hawaii**. Barack's father was also named Barack Obama. He had come to the United States from **Kenya** to go to college. He met Barack's mother, Ann Dunham, while both of them were students at the University of Hawaii.

Barack and Ann called their son Barry. The three of them lived with Ann's parents, Stanley and Madelyn. Barry called his grandfather Gramps. He called his grandmother Toot, the Hawaiian word for "grandmother."

Together, these islands make up the state of Hawaii.

Barack Obama grew up to be a
United States senator.

When Barry's father finished college, he went back to Kenya. His marriage to Ann ended. Barry's mother could not explain to him why his father had left. So Barry grew up feeling that something was missing.

When Barry was little, he spent many days at the beach. There he learned how to swim and body surf. Gramps had a friend who had a small fishing boat. The man took Gramps and Barry spear fishing in the ocean.

Sea creatures in Hawaii

This is a beach in Hawaii, near where Barry lived with his mother and grandparents.

Chapter 2

Barry's Big Adventure

In 1967, when Barry was six, his mother, Ann, married a student from **Indonesia** named Lolo Soetoro. Barry and his mother went to live in Indonesia with Lolo.

They lived near the city of **Jakarta**. In the backyard were chickens, ducks, and two baby crocodiles. They also had a pet gibbon, a tailless ape, named Tata.

Lolo took Barry and Ann to visit villages in the jungle. Barry saw boys riding on water buffalo. Barry tasted foods he had never eaten before. He tried dog meat, snake meat, and roasted grasshopper.

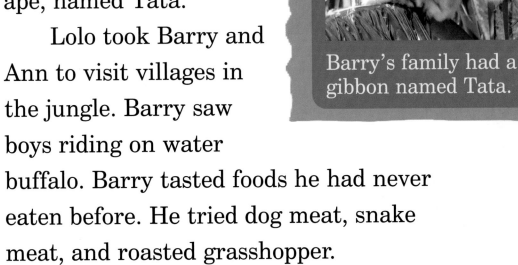

Barry's family had a gibbon named Tata.

On this map, Jakarta is marked with a star.

This is Barry's class picture from his school in Indonesia.

Barry went to school in Indonesia. He quickly learned the Indonesian language and customs. He also learned about what it means to be poor. Some Indonesians were rich, but many were very, very poor. Some people had enough to eat, while others did not know when they would eat again.

After a few years, Ann was afraid that Barry was not learning enough at school. Also, she and Lolo were not getting along very well. So in 1971, Ann and Barry moved back to Hawaii. The **adventure** was over.

Barry Visits Africa

Once again, Ann and Barry lived with Gramps and Toot in Honolulu. Ten-year-old Barry entered the fifth grade. That year, Barack, Barry's father, came from Africa to visit. He told Barry all about Africa and his relatives there. A month later Barack went home to Kenya. Barry never saw his father again.

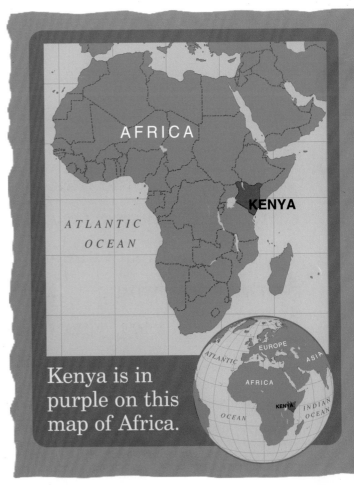

Kenya is in purple on this map of Africa.

This class picture from Barry's school in Hawaii was taken when he was about fifteen.

Barry played on the basketball team in high school.

Barry was a good student. In high school, he played on the school basketball team. To others, Barry seemed happy. But something was bothering him. Barry's mother was white. His father was black. Barry really did not know how he fit in or where he belonged. He felt different, and he felt alone.

These yearbook pictures are from Barry's senior year in high school.

WE GO PLAY HOOP

Thanks Tut, Gramps, Choom Gang, and Ray for all the good times.

Barry Obama

In 1979, Barry began studying at Occidental College in Los Angeles. While he was at college, Barry learned that South Africa had a white government that was very unfair to black people. Barry spoke out against the terrible treatment of blacks in South Africa. He began to think of himself as black. He started to call himself by his Kenyan name, Barack. He took pride in the name, which means "blessing from God."

In 1981, Barack switched to Columbia University in New York City. He graduated in 1983. For the next few years, Barack worked in Chicago helping poor people in **housing projects** make their lives better.

In 1988, Barack traveled to Kenya. There he met his grandmother, Sarah Hussein Obama, for the first time. He also met aunts, uncles, and cousins.

Barack traveled to Kenya several times. Here he is visiting a game reserve.

Sadly, Barack's father was no longer alive. Barack cried at his father's grave. By the time he left Kenya, Barack really knew who he was.

Barack with his grandmother in Kenya.

Barack Becomes a Senator

When Barack returned from Africa, he went to Harvard Law School near Boston. He graduated in 1991 with the highest honors. That same year he married Michelle Robinson, a lawyer he had met in Chicago. Later they had two daughters, Malia and Sasha.

Barack with his wife, Michelle, and his daughters Sasha (on left) and Malia (right).

In 1992, Barack began working for a law firm in Chicago. He gave legal help to people who had been treated unfairly at their jobs. Barack decided he could do the most good for the most people if he got into politics. In 1996, he won an election for Illinois state senator. For seven years, he worked to pass laws that helped the people of Illinois.

Barack watches the governor of Illinois sign a new law.

Barack Obama makes a speech to the people who are deciding who will run for president.

In 2004, Barack was elected a U.S. senator from Illinois. That same year, he gave an important speech. He said that if Americans joined together, they could make dreams come true for every parent and child.

Barack traveled all over the country making speeches and meeting people.

Barack Obama in his office in Washington, D.C. He has pictures of famous people on the wall, like Martin Luther King, Jr., and Abraham Lincoln.

In 2007, Barack Obama decided to run for president of the United States. He said that he wanted to help make America a better place for everyone.

Timeline

1961—Barack Obama (Barry) is born in Honolulu, Hawaii, on August 4.

1967—Barry moves to Jakarta, Indonesia, with his mother and stepfather, Lolo Soetoro.

1971—Barry and his mother return to Hawaii. His father visits from Africa.

1979—Barry starts college. He starts to use his full first name, Barack.

1983—Barack graduates from Columbia University in New York City.

1988—Barack travels to Kenya and meets his African grandmother and other relatives.

1991—Barack graduates from Harvard Law School. He marries Michelle Robinson.

1992—Barack begins working for a law firm in Chicago.

1996—Barack wins an election for Illinois state senator.

2004—Barack gives an important speech. Barack is elected a U.S. Senator from Illinois.

2007—Barack decides to run for president of the United States.

Learn More

Books

Doak, Robin S. *Indonesia*. Minneapolis, Minn.: Compass Point Books, 2004.

Dubois, Muriel L. *The U.S. Senate*. Mankato, Minn.: Capstone Press, 2004.

Edwards, Roberta. *Barack Obama: An American Story*. New York: Grosset & Dunlap, 2007.

Frost, Helen. *A Look at Kenya*. Mankato, Minn.: Pebble Books, 2002.

Web Sites

Barack Obama's Web Site

<http://obama.senate.gov/>

Barack Obama's Speech at the Democratic National Convention

<http://americanradioworks.publicradio.org/features/sayitplain/>

Scroll to end of list and click on "Barack Obama."

Index

Dunham, Ann (mother), 4, 6, 8, 10, 11, 13

Dunham, Madelyn (Toot), 4, 11

Dunham, Stanley (Gramps), 4, 6, 11

Harvard Law School, 17

Hawaii, 4, 6, 10, 11

Honolulu, 4, 11

Indonesia, 8–10

Jakarta, 9

Kenya, 4, 6, 11, 14, 15–16

Obama, Barack
childhood, 4, 6, 8–11
in Chicago, 14, 17, 18
education, 10, 11, 13, 14, 17
as lawyer, 18
as presidential candidate, 21
as state senator, 18
as U.S. senator, 19
visiting Kenya, 15–16

Obama, Barack (father), 4, 6, 11, 13, 16

Obama, Malia, 17

Obama, Sarah Hussein, 15

Obama, Sasha, 17

Robinson, Michelle, 17

Soetoro, Lolo, 8–9, 10

South Africa, 14

Tata (gibbon), 9